Name	
Email	

If this is not you, and you can't seem to find the original owner, **then please do the right thing** and email them with details on when, where and how they can pick it up. What you hold in your hands isn't some ordinary book or a stack of pages. **It's a piece of someone's life.** It contains personal thoughts, ambitions and goals that they have set for themselves.

This makes it just as valuable as the irreplaceable photograph you have of your grandmother, or grandfather, or a pet dog that is no longer with us. So treat it with respect, and don't be a dick-head by flipping through it or vandalizing it. We know it can be temping. But you're better than this. We believe in your humanity. Prove us right… but more importantly, prove *yourself* right.

In fact, why not take this opportunity to take your life to the next level? Do you believe things happen for a reason? We do. The fact that you stumbled upon this planner may not just be due to chance. Maybe you were *meant* to find it so you too can use a tool such as this to enhance your life.

Grab your very own copy by going to www.doyouevenhustle.net/planner and see why entrepreneurs all over the world are using it to achieve their highest-priority goals. And don't forget to email us your story here: **info@doyouevenhustle.net**

We would love to hear all about it!

Copyright © 2016 Sahil Mulla & Martin Dasko. All Rights Reserved.

Published under partnership with CreateSpace – an Amazon Company. No part of this publication may be reproduced, stored in a retrieval system or transmitted in any form or by any means (electronic, mechanical, photocopying, recording, scanning, or otherwise) without prior writer permission of the authors. Any requests to the authors or Publisher should be directed to info@doyouevenhustle.net

ISBN-13: 978-1530454242, ISBN-10: 1530454247

Limit of Liability/Disclaimer of Warranty: While the authors have used their best efforts in preparing this book, they make to representations or warranties with respect to the accuracy or completeness of the contents of this book and specifically disclaim any implied warranties of merchantability or fitness for a particular purpose. No warranty may be created or extended by sales representatives or written sales materials. The advice and strategies contained herein may not be suitable for your situation. You should consult with a professional where appropriate. Neither the publisher nor author shall be liable for any loss of profit or any other commercial damages, including but limited to special, incidental, consequential or other damages.

Contents

Why This Planner Will Succeed When All Others Have Failed You!.................. 4

The Power Of The Hand-Written Word.. 5

Two Small (But Important) Steps To Take Before You Get Started.................. 8

How To Use Your Success Planner 11

Congrats, You Made It! Here's What To Do Next…... 134

Bonus: 31 Ways To Stay Motivated.. 135

Final Thoughts 146

THE HUSTLER'S SUCCESS PLANNER

Learn How To Take Back Control Of Your Time, Boost Productivity And Achieve Your Most Audacious Goals In 60 Days Or Less!

Presented By

WWW.DOYOUEVENHUSTLE.NET

Sahil Mulla & Martin Dasko

Why This Planner <u>Will Succeed</u> When All Others Have Failed You!

Look, we get it. This isn't your first rodeo. In fact, we're well aware that you've probably tried "everything" when it comes to increasing productivity and goal setting, but nothing seems to last.

Or maybe you currently have a way of doing things, but just aren't seeing the results you want.

Either way you slice it, the fact that you bought this planner means you're *still* searching for the answer. Because if there's one thing you know, it's that there most definitely *is* a better way of doing things which exists.

I mean there *must* be, right? How else can you explain the incredible results that the top entrepreneurs of the world are getting?

Well look no further, because what you hold in your hands is a product that we created based on 3 simple principals which we've been using to smash our goals, and keep our productivity on overdrive for years.

Here Are The 3 Principals That Make It Work:

1. **It's stupidly simple;** all you have to do is fill out the blank sections we designed, every day. Your job is to leave the minimum amount of white space when it comes to organizing your day (usually takes about 10-15 minutes).

2. **It's backed by science;** we did some real research on the back-end to make sure none of our methods were hocus-pocus. You won't find any skeptical "wish your way to success" nonsense here. Like any good science experiment, the results are repeatable and reproducible.

3. **Proven in the real world;** some of the most successful people on the planet plan their day using the very same techniques you're about to learn. So why not just stand on the shoulders of giants? Why re-invent the wheel when you don't have to?

The Elephant In The Room

Let's not dodge around the underlying issue: change is annoyingly difficult. The body hates change. Change requires energy. Contrary to what you've been told, human body actually prefers homeostasis.

On top of that, we assume you're also (rightfully) skeptical about all of this. And so, you're not sure if you want to spend the energy required to adopt a completely new goal-setting system for the long haul.

But thankfully, we have some good news: the Hustler's Success Planner doesn't need you to commit for the rest of your life.

Nope, all we ask is that you trust it for the next 60 days *without* prior judgement or forming a baseless opinion about it.

This means you must be "in".

You must be committed 100%.

In fact, we almost ask that you *blindly* follow the simple system which we've created for you. No cheating, modifying, editing or changing the process in any way.

The reason for this is simple: after 60 days it will not only become a habit, but the results you see will be so dramatic, that we know you'll willingly convert to our way of doing things.

Success **itself** builds motivation when you have *momentum* on your side.

The Power Of The Hand-Written Word

You might be wondering, "if this system is so great, there must be an app that can do what this planner does!"

Well stop wondering, because there isn't. In fact, put down your phone and forget about the latest and greatest apps - they're not going to get you anywhere in life. How do we know? Because some of the most successful people that have ever lived did so without constantly typing out things on a rectangular glass screen.

What they did instead was harness the power of the written word. They did it by making sure their thoughts and ideas flowed out through their fingertips, and onto a piece of paper.

Now don't get us wrong, we love technology. After all, our main businesses would be nothing without the internet (for those that don't know, Martin runs a popular finance website called **Studanomics.com**, and Sahil has his own fitness company over at **HardcoreTrainingSolutions.com**).

On top of this, we host a thriving podcast to boot (it recently hit the "new & noteworthy" list in iTunes).

So why didn't we do what every other young entrepreneur is doing and design an app for you to download? Why did we choose this archaic method of writing things down when it comes to planning your day?

Because this isn't about being cool, or controversial, or different. This is about being **effective**. And the most effective and successful entrepreneurs write things down, and are in total control of their day. Also, it's about **not** reinventing the wheel. Smart phones, tablets and laptops are actually a pretty recent invention if you think about it. Clearly, we had successful individuals that were running large multi-national corporations back in the day.

So how did they stay on top of their shit without high-end technology?

Well, we believe the good ol' paper had a lot to do with it. And as it turns out, science is on the side of the hand-written word as well. Research has shown that writing things down has plenty of advantages over typing. Here are a few:

- **Better focus.** Because you have to take your time, writing things down with a pen zones you in. It's not like you can open a new app or tab in your browser and check your email. Nor can you see what your friends have been up to on Facebook.

- **Better memory.** Indiana University did a survey of their students, and found that those who took notes by hand had a better time recalling facts, and generally a had higher academic average than their typing counterparts.

- **Faster learning.** I remember reading an article in the Wall Street

Journal which talked about a study in which adults were asked to learn new symbols and shapes. As it turns out, those that actually wrote them down by hand, learned and retained the new information at a much faster pace.

- **Sparks creativity**. While no one is saying a keyboard will make you boring, uncreative and stupid, we've found that writing things down by hand simply gives you an edge because of the freedom and flexibility it provides. You can create diagrams, symbols, sketches and format things the way you wish. Why do you think Apple created a stylus? Or the reason why Samsung's Note sells so well?

We could go on and on, but feel that the point has been made – when it comes to doing something important - such as organizing your freakin' life - you should opt for the pen (and this success planner, of course).

In fact, organizing your day with this planner may be the only time in your day when you actually end up having to write something by hand, which means you might feel slow and clumsy. But that's ok, because you'll actually become a better writer and note-taker if you stick with it for the next 60 days.

Two Small (But Important) Steps To Take Before You Get Started

Step 1: Go On An Information Diet

Get rid of (or put away) your useless old agenda, wall calendar, sticky note stack, to-do list and everything else you currently use. Those are now considered distractions. Keep this planner close to your heart. Treat it like a monogamous relationship. Carry it with you everywhere, and we promise it will deliver!

If you're having anxiety at the thought of removing distractions from your life, then there are two things you can do to keep that inner hoarder happy.

For digital files and apps, back them up and save them in a .zip format, inside of a folder that you can always revisit at a later date.

Smart phone apps that you've paid for can be uninstalled and reinstalled at any time.

For physical things, box them up and store them away. We can't emphasize how important it is to stay true to this planner as your sole source of organization and motivation.

Step 2: Figure Out Your Core Motivator

"He who has a why can endure any how." – Frederick Nietzsche

Do you have a real reason for wanting to accomplish your biggest goals? Or are you doing it because it's the "cool" thing to do?

What's your "why"?

This step is so important, that we dedicated an entire episode on our podcast to it (episode 3). What this concept boils down to is figuring out your purpose. You can always figure out the who, what, where, and when later. In fact, those things are *easy*. We can help you with those any day of the week. But finding your why is difficult because you have strip everything down, and figure out what your *true* reasoning is. You have to do some real soul-searching.

Your why not only wakes you up in the morning, but it's what will drive you forward with serious momentum till you take your last breath. Your why is your competitive advantage. Your why is the reason behind everything that you do. Your why affects every action you will ever take.

We've thrown in some questions to help fire up your creativity, and help you come up with your **why**. DO NOT skip this step until you've figured it out.

It might take you hours to find your exact WHY. That's okay. Take your time. This may end up being an emotional rollercoaster of a ride. We really want you to dig deep here. Trust us, the work is worth it!

If you had all the money in the world, write down a few things you would still continue to do daily. *(e.g Sahil & Martin would still continue to run the DYEH podcast, and produce content for their audience and customers)*

_____

_____

_____

_____

If someone placed a gun to your head, and *forced* you to choose one profession and/or career path for the rest of your life, what would it be and why?

_____

_____

_____

_____

When your great grandchildren look back to research what you were all about, what would you like them to find? What type of legacy would you like to leave behind? How do you want them to remember you?

_____

_____

_____

_____

_____

_____

_____

_____

Based on the answers from the reflections you've written earlier, come up with your why statement (or multiple why statements).

_____

_____

_____

_____

_____

_____

You'll be reviewing and writing down your "why" statement(s) on a daily basis, so be sure to memorize them. For now, let's talk about how to actually use this planner…

How To Use Your Success Planner

Each day has been assigned two pages. The first page is designed to accomplish a multitude of things such as:

i) Motivate you with a unique quote of the day
ii) Re-align you with your goals
iii) Get your mind working in a positive state

You'll also be jump-starting your creativity so you can come up with unique solutions to problems that you may encounter during your day. Let's take a moment to go over each section:

List 3 Things You're Grateful For Today

Regardless of your situation, someone out there has it worse. And so this section is aimed to get you thinking positively. Even if you think you have nothing, I'm sure you can find something to be grateful for. Do you have a roof over your head? This planner in your hands? A connection to the internet? These are all very real things to be genuinely grateful for.

Your Top 5 Long Term Goals (1-3 Years)

Forget being "realistic". This is your time to dream. Your time to let your imagination fly. You want to become a NY Times best seller? Write it down. You want to start a multi-national corporation? Great, write that down as well. Don't let anyone tell you that your goals are "unrealistic". In fact, we say **be unreasonable**. Take the goal you want, then 5x, 10x or even 15x it.

Take a moment to think about this: Would you rather fall shy of hitting an income goal of $10 million, or falling shy of just $100,000?

Yeah we thought so. Also, if it feels redundant to write down the same goals every day, then our suggestion for you is to stop judging the process. Most people write down their goals once, maybe twice in a year. Most never even look at them again. Some may reflect or review them, but that's weak. Think about it, who is more likely to accomplish their goals: the person that writes them down over 300 times a year, or someone that writes them down once or twice? Exactly.

Plus, your goals **do not** need to be set in stone. In fact, you'll find that they evolve over time. Being a NY Times best seller may morph into *"sell 100,000 copies of my book"* because you realized you couldn't give a shit about an arbitrary badge of recognition – you're out to make some serious BANK, and if the sales numbers are high enough, you'll make that list anyway. Perfect.

Just be careful to not become too distracted and indecisive. You don't want to be the person that completely changes their goals every few days. That's like setting a completely different GPS destination every 10 minutes... how can you expect to get anywhere?!

The 5 Things You Aim To Accomplish Today

So while we previously asked you to dream big and keep your head amongst the clouds, now it's time to get back down to Earth. This is the section where you will need to be grounded. Write down the five *very realistic* and meaningful tasks you want to accomplish today. Tasks that will inch you closer to your goals.

They can't be too easy (like brushing your teeth), nor can they be too hard (close a $5 million dollar deal by cold calling the CEO of Spotify). However, something like *"email the CEO of Spotify & ask for a meeting"* would definitely fit the bill. You get to dictate what feels meaningful to you.

If you have more than five, put them on the back burner right now. Or prioritize, and write down the five which are the *most* important. Once you have your five, immediately schedule them into your daily time table. You'll also notice an extra column to the right. This is where you "check off" the tasks or missions once they are completed. **If you failed to complete a task**, we suggest you carry it forward to the next day (if applicable).

Come Up With 5 Unique Ideas

This is the section where we stress your creative muscle. If you're new to this, your might have a sluggish start for the first few days. In fact, you might dread this section every day for the first week or so. But keep at it, and soon things will flip.

As your creative muscle gets stronger, your ideas will rise in quality. You'll find yourself coming up with nuggets of real brilliance. You'll also come up with some utterly stupid shit, but that's ok! When it comes to this section, there are only two rules that apply:

1. **Do not judge your ideas;** *"start a nude lemon-aid stand"* is just as viable as *"write a book on changing brake pads and give it away to the readers of MotorTrend magazine."* Also, no one said the ideas had to be business related. Maybe you want to duct-tape your toaster to a wall so that slices of bread fly out and land on a plate every morning. Great, write it down! Just because it's an idea, doesn't mean you need to execute it (yet).

2. **You cannot repeat ideas;** they must be unique. If you're really stuck, you can change some parameters from the previous days. Going of the example above, you could write something like: *"start a nude bakery."* But you'd only be cheating yourself. Try and push your creative boundaries a little!

End Of The Day Reflections

Regardless of how good or bad your day went, the one thing we know for sure is that life always has a way of hurling meaningful lessons your way. The key is to listen, and pay attention. If you're too busy "talking" or indulging in the noise, you will miss out. So this section is for you to fill out before you wrap it in for the night. Take a few minutes and write down any and all take-away lessons that you picked up on.

Maybe you had a major fuck-up at work today… if so, this is the perfect opportunity to extract a lesson from it. Every big failure comes with an equally jumbo-sized life lesson. On the other hand, every success comes with a nugget of gold as well. It's *your* job to find these nuggets. And the only way to do that is to sit down, without distractions, and reflect.

Quote Of The Day
"Give me six hours to chop down a tree and I will spend the first four sharpening the axe." – Abraham Lincoln

List 3 Things You're Grateful For Today

1	
2	
3	

Your Top 5 Long Term Goals (1-3 Years)

1	
2	
3	
4	
5	

The 5 Things You Aim To Accomplish Today

1		
2		
3		
4		
5		

Come Up With 5 Unique Ideas

1	
2	
3	
4	
5	

End Of The Day Reflections

Plan Out Your Day | Today's Date:

What's Your Why

_____
_____
_____

What do Elon Musk, Oprah, and a broke loser complaining about not finding a job have in common? They each get only 24 hours in a day. And so do you. So be sure to spend yours wisely!

12am	
1	
2	
3	
4	
5	
6	
7	
8	
9	
10	
11	
12pm	
1	
2	
3	
4	
5	
6	
7	
8	
9	
10	
11	

Quote Of The Day

"If you want to know your past, look into your present conditions. If you want to know your future, look into your present actions." – Chinese Proverb

List 3 Things You're Grateful For Today

1	
2	
3	

Your Top 5 Long Term Goals (1-3 Years)

1	
2	
3	
4	
5	

The 5 Things You Aim To Accomplish Today

1		
2		
3		
4		
5		

Come Up With 5 Unique Ideas

1	
2	
3	
4	
5	

End Of The Day Reflections

_____

_____

_____

_____

_____

Plan Out Your Day | Today's Date:

What's Your Why

_____
_____
_____

What do Elon Musk, Oprah, and a broke loser complaining about not finding a job have in common? They each get only 24 hours in a day. And so do you. So be sure to spend yours wisely!

12am	
1	
2	
3	
4	
5	
6	
7	
8	
9	
10	
11	
12pm	
1	
2	
3	
4	
5	
6	
7	
8	
9	
10	
11	

Quote Of The Day

"Fuck em! They need to talk about you to get attention because if they end up talking about themselves, no one would give a shit" – Shia Labeouf

List 3 Things You're Grateful For Today

1	
2	
3	

Your Top 5 Long Term Goals (1-3 Years)

1	
2	
3	
4	
5	

The 5 Things You Aim To Accomplish Today

1		
2		
3		
4		
5		

Come Up With 5 Unique Ideas

1	
2	
3	
4	
5	

End Of The Day Reflections

_____
_____
_____
_____
_____
_____

Plan Out Your Day | Today's Date:

What's Your Why

_____
_____
_____

What do Elon Musk, Oprah, and a broke loser complaining about not finding a job have in common? They each get only 24 hours in a day. And so do you. So be sure to spend yours wisely!

12am	
1	
2	
3	
4	
5	
6	
7	
8	
9	
10	
11	
12pm	
1	
2	
3	
4	
5	
6	
7	
8	
9	
10	
11	

Quote Of The Day
"Ordinary actions repeated over a period of time, produce extra-ordinary results" - Unknown

List 3 Things You're Grateful For Today

1	
2	
3	

Your Top 5 Long Term Goals (1-3 Years)

1	
2	
3	
4	
5	

The 5 Things You Aim To Accomplish Today

1		
2		
3		
4		
5		

Come Up With 5 Unique Ideas

1	
2	
3	
4	
5	

End Of The Day Reflections

_____
_____
_____
_____
_____

Plan Out Your Day | Today's Date:

What's Your Why

_____
_____
_____

What do Elon Musk, Oprah, and a broke loser complaining about not finding a job have in common? They each get only 24 hours in a day. And so do you. So be sure to spend yours wisely!

12am	
1	
2	
3	
4	
5	
6	
7	
8	
9	
10	
11	
12pm	
1	
2	
3	
4	
5	
6	
7	
8	
9	
10	
11	

Quote Of The Day
"Unless you pay the price for success, you will not know its worth"– Apoorve Dubey

List 3 Things You're Grateful For Today

1	
2	
3	

Your Top 5 Long Term Goals (1-3 Years)

1	
2	
3	
4	
5	

The 5 Things You Aim To Accomplish Today

1		
2		
3		
4		
5		

Come Up With 5 Unique Ideas

1	
2	
3	
4	
5	

End Of The Day Reflections

_____
_____
_____
_____
_____
_____

Plan Out Your Day | Today's Date:

What's Your Why

_____
_____
_____

What do Elon Musk, Oprah, and a broke loser complaining about not finding a job have in common? They each get only 24 hours in a day. And so do you. So be sure to spend yours wisely!

12am	
1	
2	
3	
4	
5	
6	
7	
8	
9	
10	
11	
12pm	
1	
2	
3	
4	
5	
6	
7	
8	
9	
10	
11	

Quote Of The Day
"What you get by achieving your goals is not as important as what you become by achieving your goals." – Henry David Thoreau

List 3 Things You're Grateful For Today

1	
2	
3	

Your Top 5 Long Term Goals (1-3 Years)

1	
2	
3	
4	
5	

The 5 Things You Aim To Accomplish Today

1		
2		
3		
4		
5		

Come Up With 5 Unique Ideas

1	
2	
3	
4	
5	

End Of The Day Reflections

_____
_____
_____
_____
_____

Plan Out Your Day | Today's Date:

What's Your Why

_____
_____
_____

What do Elon Musk, Oprah, and a broke loser complaining about not finding a job have in common? They each get only 24 hours in a day. And so do you. So be sure to spend yours wisely!

12am	
1	
2	
3	
4	
5	
6	
7	
8	
9	
10	
11	
12pm	
1	
2	
3	
4	
5	
6	
7	
8	
9	
10	
11	

Quote Of The Day

"I hate how many people think their glass is half-empty when their glass is really four-fifths full. I'm grateful when I have one drop in the glass because I know exactly what to do with it." – Gary Vaynerchuk

List 3 Things You're Grateful For Today

1	
2	
3	

Your Top 5 Long Term Goals (1-3 Years)

1	
2	
3	
4	
5	

The 5 Things You Aim To Accomplish Today

1		
2		
3		
4		
5		

Come Up With 5 Unique Ideas

1	
2	
3	
4	
5	

End Of The Day Reflections

Plan Out Your Day | Today's Date:

What's Your Why

_____
_____
_____

What do Elon Musk, Oprah, and a broke loser complaining about not finding a job have in common? They each get only 24 hours in a day. And so do you. So be sure to spend yours wisely!

12am	
1	
2	
3	
4	
5	
6	
7	
8	
9	
10	
11	
12pm	
1	
2	
3	
4	
5	
6	
7	
8	
9	
10	
11	

Quote Of The Day
"A pessimist is someone who complains about the noise when opportunity comes knocking" – Oscar Wilde

List 3 Things You're Grateful For Today

1	
2	
3	

Your Top 5 Long Term Goals (1-3 Years)

1	
2	
3	
4	
5	

The 5 Things You Aim To Accomplish Today

1		
2		
3		
4		
5		

Come Up With 5 Unique Ideas

1	
2	
3	
4	
5	

End Of The Day Reflections

Plan Out Your Day | Today's Date:

What's Your Why

_____
_____
_____

What do Elon Musk, Oprah, and a broke loser complaining about not finding a job have in common? They each get only 24 hours in a day. And so do you. So be sure to spend yours wisely!

12am	
1	
2	
3	
4	
5	
6	
7	
8	
9	
10	
11	
12pm	
1	
2	
3	
4	
5	
6	
7	
8	
9	
10	
11	

Quote Of The Day
"Have goals so big, that you get uncomfortable telling small minded people"
- Unknown

List 3 Things You're Grateful For Today

#	
1	
2	
3	

Your Top 5 Long Term Goals (1-3 Years)

#	
1	
2	
3	
4	
5	

The 5 Things You Aim To Accomplish Today

#		
1		
2		
3		
4		
5		

Come Up With 5 Unique Ideas

#	
1	
2	
3	
4	
5	

End Of The Day Reflections

Plan Out Your Day | Today's Date:

What's Your Why

_____
_____
_____

What do Elon Musk, Oprah, and a broke loser complaining about not finding a job have in common? They each get only 24 hours in a day. And so do you. So be sure to spend yours wisely!

12am	
1	
2	
3	
4	
5	
6	
7	
8	
9	
10	
11	
12pm	
1	
2	
3	
4	
5	
6	
7	
8	
9	
10	
11	

Quote Of The Day

"One day the view from the top will be worth all the hustle you put in while you were at the bottom" – DoYouEvenHustle Podcast

List 3 Things You're Grateful For Today

1	
2	
3	

Your Top 5 Long Term Goals (1-3 Years)

1	
2	
3	
4	
5	

The 5 Things You Aim To Accomplish Today

1		
2		
3		
4		
5		

Come Up With 5 Unique Ideas

1	
2	
3	
4	
5	

End Of The Day Reflections

Plan Out Your Day | Today's Date:

What's Your Why

_____
_____
_____

What do Elon Musk, Oprah, and a broke loser complaining about not finding a job have in common? They each get only 24 hours in a day. And so do you. So be sure to spend yours wisely!

12am	
1	
2	
3	
4	
5	
6	
7	
8	
9	
10	
11	
12pm	
1	
2	
3	
4	
5	
6	
7	
8	
9	
10	
11	

Quote Of The Day
"Better to be a diamond with a flaw than a pebble without one" – Confucius

List 3 Things You're Grateful For Today

1	
2	
3	

Your Top 5 Long Term Goals (1-3 Years)

1	
2	
3	
4	
5	

The 5 Things You Aim To Accomplish Today

1		
2		
3		
4		
5		

Come Up With 5 Unique Ideas

1	
2	
3	
4	
5	

End Of The Day Reflections

_____

_____

_____

_____

_____

Plan Out Your Day | Today's Date:

What's Your Why

_____
_____
_____

What do Elon Musk, Oprah, and a broke loser complaining about not finding a job have in common? They each get only 24 hours in a day. And so do you. So be sure to spend yours wisely!

12am	
1	
2	
3	
4	
5	
6	
7	
8	
9	
10	
11	
12pm	
1	
2	
3	
4	
5	
6	
7	
8	
9	
10	
11	

Quote Of The Day
"Do you know why we fall, sir? So that we may learn to pick ourselves back up!" – Alfred from Batman Begins

List 3 Things You're Grateful For Today

1	
2	
3	

Your Top 5 Long Term Goals (1-3 Years)

1	
2	
3	
4	
5	

The 5 Things You Aim To Accomplish Today

1		
2		
3		
4		
5		

Come Up With 5 Unique Ideas

1	
2	
3	
4	
5	

End Of The Day Reflections

Plan Out Your Day | Today's Date:

What's Your Why

_____
_____
_____

What do Elon Musk, Oprah, and a broke loser complaining about not finding a job have in common? They each get only 24 hours in a day. And so do you. So be sure to spend yours wisely!

12am	
1	
2	
3	
4	
5	
6	
7	
8	
9	
10	
11	
12pm	
1	
2	
3	
4	
5	
6	
7	
8	
9	
10	
11	

Quote Of The Day
"How many success stories do you need to hear before deciding to make your own?" - Unknown

List 3 Things You're Grateful For Today

1	
2	
3	

Your Top 5 Long Term Goals (1-3 Years)

1	
2	
3	
4	
5	

The 5 Things You Aim To Accomplish Today

1		
2		
3		
4		
5		

Come Up With 5 Unique Ideas

1	
2	
3	
4	
5	

End Of The Day Reflections

_____
_____
_____
_____
_____
_____

Plan Out Your Day | Today's Date:

What's Your Why

_____
_____
_____

What do Elon Musk, Oprah, and a broke loser complaining about not finding a job have in common? They each get only 24 hours in a day. And so do you. So be sure to spend yours wisely!

12am	
1	
2	
3	
4	
5	
6	
7	
8	
9	
10	
11	
12pm	
1	
2	
3	
4	
5	
6	
7	
8	
9	
10	
11	

Quote Of The Day

"Pain is temporary; it may last for a minute, or an hour, or a day, or even a year. But eventually it will subside, but something else will take it's place. If you quit however, it will last forever." – Eric Thomas

List 3 Things You're Grateful For Today

1	
2	
3	

Your Top 5 Long Term Goals (1-3 Years)

1	
2	
3	
4	
5	

The 5 Things You Aim To Accomplish Today

1		
2		
3		
4		
5		

Come Up With 5 Unique Ideas

1	
2	
3	
4	
5	

End Of The Day Reflections

_____
_____
_____
_____
_____

Plan Out Your Day | Today's Date:

What's Your Why

_____
_____
_____

What do Elon Musk, Oprah, and a broke loser complaining about not finding a job have in common? They each get only 24 hours in a day. And so do you. So be sure to spend yours wisely!

12am	
1	
2	
3	
4	
5	
6	
7	
8	
9	
10	
11	
12pm	
1	
2	
3	
4	
5	
6	
7	
8	
9	
10	
11	

Quote Of The Day
"Tears may get you sympathy, but sweat will get you results" – Unknown

List 3 Things You're Grateful For Today

1	
2	
3	

Your Top 5 Long Term Goals (1-3 Years)

1	
2	
3	
4	
5	

The 5 Things You Aim To Accomplish Today

1		
2		
3		
4		
5		

Come Up With 5 Unique Ideas

1	
2	
3	
4	
5	

End Of The Day Reflections

Plan Out Your Day | Today's Date:

What's Your Why

_____
_____
_____

What do Elon Musk, Oprah, and a broke loser complaining about not finding a job have in common? They each get only 24 hours in a day. And so do you. So be sure to spend yours wisely!

12am	
1	
2	
3	
4	
5	
6	
7	
8	
9	
10	
11	
12pm	
1	
2	
3	
4	
5	
6	
7	
8	
9	
10	
11	

Quote Of The Day
"You can't push yourself forward by patting your own ass" - Sahil Mulla

List 3 Things You're Grateful For Today

1	
2	
3	

Your Top 5 Long Term Goals (1-3 Years)

1	
2	
3	
4	
5	

The 5 Things You Aim To Accomplish Today

1		
2		
3		
4		
5		

Come Up With 5 Unique Ideas

1	
2	
3	
4	
5	

End Of The Day Reflections

_____
_____
_____
_____
_____

Plan Out Your Day | Today's Date:

What's Your Why

_____
_____
_____

What do Elon Musk, Oprah, and a broke loser complaining about not finding a job have in common? They each get only 24 hours in a day. And so do you. So be sure to spend yours wisely!

12am	
1	
2	
3	
4	
5	
6	
7	
8	
9	
10	
11	
12pm	
1	
2	
3	
4	
5	
6	
7	
8	
9	
10	
11	

Quote Of The Day

"Success and failure. We think of them as opposites, but they're really not. They're companions, the hero and the sidekick." – Laurence Shames

List 3 Things You're Grateful For Today

1	
2	
3	

Your Top 5 Long Term Goals (1-3 Years)

1	
2	
3	
4	
5	

The 5 Things You Aim To Accomplish Today

1		
2		
3		
4		
5		

Come Up With 5 Unique Ideas

1	
2	
3	
4	
5	

End Of The Day Reflections

_____
_____
_____
_____
_____

Plan Out Your Day | Today's Date:

What's Your Why

_____
_____
_____

What do Elon Musk, Oprah, and a broke loser complaining about not finding a job have in common? They each get only 24 hours in a day. And so do you. So be sure to spend yours wisely!

12am	
1	
2	
3	
4	
5	
6	
7	
8	
9	
10	
11	
12pm	
1	
2	
3	
4	
5	
6	
7	
8	
9	
10	
11	

Quote Of The Day
"If people are talking behind your back, it's only because you're ahead of them" – Unknown

List 3 Things You're Grateful For Today

1
2
3

Your Top 5 Long Term Goals (1-3 Years)

1
2
3
4
5

The 5 Things You Aim To Accomplish Today

1	
2	
3	
4	
5	

Come Up With 5 Unique Ideas

1
2
3
4
5

End Of The Day Reflections

_____

_____

_____

_____

_____

Plan Out Your Day | Today's Date:

What's Your Why

_____
_____
_____

What do Elon Musk, Oprah, and a broke loser complaining about not finding a job have in common? They each get only 24 hours in a day. And so do you. So be sure to spend yours wisely!

12am	
1	
2	
3	
4	
5	
6	
7	
8	
9	
10	
11	
12pm	
1	
2	
3	
4	
5	
6	
7	
8	
9	
10	
11	

Quote Of The Day
"Be a yardstick of quality. Some people aren't used to an environment where excellence is expected." – Steve Jobs

List 3 Things You're Grateful For Today

1	
2	
3	

Your Top 5 Long Term Goals (1-3 Years)

1	
2	
3	
4	
5	

The 5 Things You Aim To Accomplish Today

1		
2		
3		
4		
5		

Come Up With 5 Unique Ideas

1	
2	
3	
4	
5	

End Of The Day Reflections

_____
_____
_____
_____
_____

Plan Out Your Day | Today's Date:

What's Your Why

_____
_____
_____

What do Elon Musk, Oprah, and a broke loser complaining about not finding a job have in common? They each get only 24 hours in a day. And so do you. So be sure to spend yours wisely!

12am	
1	
2	
3	
4	
5	
6	
7	
8	
9	
10	
11	
12pm	
1	
2	
3	
4	
5	
6	
7	
8	
9	
10	
11	

Quote Of The Day
"Fear is the interest you pay on a debt you may not even owe" - Unknown

List 3 Things You're Grateful For Today

1	
2	
3	

Your Top 5 Long Term Goals (1-3 Years)

1	
2	
3	
4	
5	

The 5 Things You Aim To Accomplish Today

1		
2		
3		
4		
5		

Come Up With 5 Unique Ideas

1	
2	
3	
4	
5	

End Of The Day Reflections

_____
_____
_____
_____
_____

Plan Out Your Day | Today's Date:

What's Your Why

_____
_____
_____

What do Elon Musk, Oprah, and a broke loser complaining about not finding a job have in common? They each get only 24 hours in a day. And so do you. So be sure to spend yours wisely!

12am	
1	
2	
3	
4	
5	
6	
7	
8	
9	
10	
11	
12pm	
1	
2	
3	
4	
5	
6	
7	
8	
9	
10	
11	

Quote Of The Day
"Don't be angry at the results you don't have with the work you didn't do" - Unknown

List 3 Things You're Grateful For Today

1	
2	
3	

Your Top 5 Long Term Goals (1-3 Years)

1	
2	
3	
4	
5	

The 5 Things You Aim To Accomplish Today

1		
2		
3		
4		
5		

Come Up With 5 Unique Ideas

1	
2	
3	
4	
5	

End Of The Day Reflections

_____

_____

_____

_____

_____

Plan Out Your Day | Today's Date:

What's Your Why

_____
_____
_____

What do Elon Musk, Oprah, and a broke loser complaining about not finding a job have in common? They each get only 24 hours in a day. And so do you. So be sure to spend yours wisely!

12am	
1	
2	
3	
4	
5	
6	
7	
8	
9	
10	
11	
12pm	
1	
2	
3	
4	
5	
6	
7	
8	
9	
10	
11	

Quote Of The Day
"The best time to plant a tree you want, was 20 years ago. The second best time is right now"– Chinese Proverb

List 3 Things You're Grateful For Today

1	
2	
3	

Your Top 5 Long Term Goals (1-3 Years)

1	
2	
3	
4	
5	

The 5 Things You Aim To Accomplish Today

1		
2		
3		
4		
5		

Come Up With 5 Unique Ideas

1	
2	
3	
4	
5	

End Of The Day Reflections

_____
_____
_____
_____
_____

Plan Out Your Day | Today's Date:

What's Your Why

_____
_____
_____

What do Elon Musk, Oprah, and a broke loser complaining about not finding a job have in common? They each get only 24 hours in a day. And so do you. So be sure to spend yours wisely!

12am	
1	
2	
3	
4	
5	
6	
7	
8	
9	
10	
11	
12pm	
1	
2	
3	
4	
5	
6	
7	
8	
9	
10	
11	

Quote Of The Day
"Challenges are what make life interesting, and overcoming them is what makes life meaningful." – Joshua J. Marine

List 3 Things You're Grateful For Today

1	
2	
3	

Your Top 5 Long Term Goals (1-3 Years)

1	
2	
3	
4	
5	

The 5 Things You Aim To Accomplish Today

1		
2		
3		
4		
5		

Come Up With 5 Unique Ideas

1	
2	
3	
4	
5	

End Of The Day Reflections

_____
_____
_____
_____
_____
_____

Plan Out Your Day | Today's Date:

What's Your Why

_____
_____
_____

What do Elon Musk, Oprah, and a broke loser complaining about not finding a job have in common? They each get only 24 hours in a day. And so do you. So be sure to spend yours wisely!

12am	
1	
2	
3	
4	
5	
6	
7	
8	
9	
10	
11	
12pm	
1	
2	
3	
4	
5	
6	
7	
8	
9	
10	
11	

Quote Of The Day

"The person who says it cannot be done should not interrupt the person who's doing it" – Chinese Proverb

List 3 Things You're Grateful For Today

1	
2	
3	

Your Top 5 Long Term Goals (1-3 Years)

1	
2	
3	
4	
5	

The 5 Things You Aim To Accomplish Today

1		
2		
3		
4		
5		

Come Up With 5 Unique Ideas

1	
2	
3	
4	
5	

End Of The Day Reflections

_____
_____
_____
_____
_____

Plan Out Your Day | Today's Date:

What's Your Why

_____
_____
_____

What do Elon Musk, Oprah, and a broke loser complaining about not finding a job have in common? They each get only 24 hours in a day. And so do you. So be sure to spend yours wisely!

12am	
1	
2	
3	
4	
5	
6	
7	
8	
9	
10	
11	
12pm	
1	
2	
3	
4	
5	
6	
7	
8	
9	
10	
11	

Quote Of The Day

"You need a plan of action. No one becomes an astronaut by accident!" – Keith Ferrazzi

List 3 Things You're Grateful For Today

1	
2	
3	

Your Top 5 Long Term Goals (1-3 Years)

1	
2	
3	
4	
5	

The 5 Things You Aim To Accomplish Today

1		
2		
3		
4		
5		

Come Up With 5 Unique Ideas

1	
2	
3	
4	
5	

End Of The Day Reflections

_____
_____
_____
_____
_____

Plan Out Your Day | Today's Date:

What's Your Why

_____
_____
_____

What do Elon Musk, Oprah, and a broke loser complaining about not finding a job have in common? They each get only 24 hours in a day. And so do you. So be sure to spend yours wisely!

12am	
1	
2	
3	
4	
5	
6	
7	
8	
9	
10	
11	
12pm	
1	
2	
3	
4	
5	
6	
7	
8	
9	
10	
11	

Quote Of The Day
"I hated every minute of training, but I said, 'Don't quit. Suffer now and live the rest of your life as a champion.'" – Muhammad Ali

List 3 Things You're Grateful For Today

1	
2	
3	

Your Top 5 Long Term Goals (1-3 Years)

1	
2	
3	
4	
5	

The 5 Things You Aim To Accomplish Today

1		
2		
3		
4		
5		

Come Up With 5 Unique Ideas

1	
2	
3	
4	
5	

End Of The Day Reflections

Plan Out Your Day | Today's Date:

What's Your Why

_____
_____
_____

What do Elon Musk, Oprah, and a broke loser complaining about not finding a job have in common? They each get only 24 hours in a day. And so do you. So be sure to spend yours wisely!

12am	
1	
2	
3	
4	
5	
6	
7	
8	
9	
10	
11	
12pm	
1	
2	
3	
4	
5	
6	
7	
8	
9	
10	
11	

Quote Of The Day

"Talent is God given. Be humble. Fame is man-given. Be grateful. Conceit is self-given. Be careful." – John Wooden

List 3 Things You're Grateful For Today

1	
2	
3	

Your Top 5 Long Term Goals (1-3 Years)

1	
2	
3	
4	
5	

The 5 Things You Aim To Accomplish Today

1		
2		
3		
4		
5		

Come Up With 5 Unique Ideas

1	
2	
3	
4	
5	

End Of The Day Reflections

Plan Out Your Day | Today's Date:

What's Your Why

_____
_____
_____

What do Elon Musk, Oprah, and a broke loser complaining about not finding a job have in common? They each get only 24 hours in a day. And so do you. So be sure to spend yours wisely!

12am	
1	
2	
3	
4	
5	
6	
7	
8	
9	
10	
11	
12pm	
1	
2	
3	
4	
5	
6	
7	
8	
9	
10	
11	

Quote Of The Day
"If you are persistent, you will get it. If you are consistent, you will keep it." – Unknown

List 3 Things You're Grateful For Today

1	
2	
3	

Your Top 5 Long Term Goals (1-3 Years)

1	
2	
3	
4	
5	

The 5 Things You Aim To Accomplish Today

1		
2		
3		
4		
5		

Come Up With 5 Unique Ideas

1	
2	
3	
4	
5	

End Of The Day Reflections

_____
_____
_____
_____
_____

Plan Out Your Day | Today's Date:

What's Your Why

_____
_____
_____

What do Elon Musk, Oprah, and a broke loser complaining about not finding a job have in common? They each get only 24 hours in a day. And so do you. So be sure to spend yours wisely!

12am	
1	
2	
3	
4	
5	
6	
7	
8	
9	
10	
11	
12pm	
1	
2	
3	
4	
5	
6	
7	
8	
9	
10	
11	

Quote Of The Day
"You sleep like you're rich, I'm up like I'm broke!" - Grant Cardone

List 3 Things You're Grateful For Today

1	
2	
3	

Your Top 5 Long Term Goals (1-3 Years)

1	
2	
3	
4	
5	

The 5 Things You Aim To Accomplish Today

1		
2		
3		
4		
5		

Come Up With 5 Unique Ideas

1	
2	
3	
4	
5	

End Of The Day Reflections

_____
_____
_____
_____
_____

Plan Out Your Day | Today's Date:

What's Your Why

_____
_____
_____

What do Elon Musk, Oprah, and a broke loser complaining about not finding a job have in common? They each get only 24 hours in a day. And so do you. So be sure to spend yours wisely!

12am	
1	
2	
3	
4	
5	
6	
7	
8	
9	
10	
11	
12pm	
1	
2	
3	
4	
5	
6	
7	
8	
9	
10	
11	

Quote Of The Day
"Without HUSTLE, talent will only carry you so far" - Gary Vaynerchuk

List 3 Things You're Grateful For Today

1	
2	
3	

Your Top 5 Long Term Goals (1-3 Years)

1	
2	
3	
4	
5	

The 5 Things You Aim To Accomplish Today

1		
2		
3		
4		
5		

Come Up With 5 Unique Ideas

1	
2	
3	
4	
5	

End Of The Day Reflections

_____
_____
_____
_____
_____

Plan Out Your Day | Today's Date:

What's Your Why

_____
_____
_____

What do Elon Musk, Oprah, and a broke loser complaining about not finding a job have in common? They each get only 24 hours in a day. And so do you. So be sure to spend yours wisely!

12am	
1	
2	
3	
4	
5	
6	
7	
8	
9	
10	
11	
12pm	
1	
2	
3	
4	
5	
6	
7	
8	
9	
10	
11	

Quote Of The Day
"A lack of play should be treated like malnutrition: it's a health risk to your body and mind." - Stuart Brow

List 3 Things You're Grateful For Today

1
2
3

Your Top 5 Long Term Goals (1-3 Years)

1
2
3
4
5

The 5 Things You Aim To Accomplish Today

1	
2	
3	
4	
5	

Come Up With 5 Unique Ideas

1
2
3
4
5

End Of The Day Reflections

Plan Out Your Day | Today's Date:

What's Your Why

_____
_____
_____

What do Elon Musk, Oprah, and a broke loser complaining about not finding a job have in common? They each get only 24 hours in a day. And so do you. So be sure to spend yours wisely!

12am	
1	
2	
3	
4	
5	
6	
7	
8	
9	
10	
11	
12pm	
1	
2	
3	
4	
5	
6	
7	
8	
9	
10	
11	

Quote Of The Day
"Man cannot discover new oceans unless he has the courage to lose sight of the shore." - Andre Gide

List 3 Things You're Grateful For Today

1	
2	
3	

Your Top 5 Long Term Goals (1-3 Years)

1	
2	
3	
4	
5	

The 5 Things You Aim To Accomplish Today

1		
2		
3		
4		
5		

Come Up With 5 Unique Ideas

1	
2	
3	
4	
5	

End Of The Day Reflections

_____

_____

_____

_____

_____

Plan Out Your Day | Today's Date:

What's Your Why

_____
_____
_____

What do Elon Musk, Oprah, and a broke loser complaining about not finding a job have in common? They each get only 24 hours in a day. And so do you. So be sure to spend yours wisely!

12am	
1	
2	
3	
4	
5	
6	
7	
8	
9	
10	
11	
12pm	
1	
2	
3	
4	
5	
6	
7	
8	
9	
10	
11	

Quote Of The Day
"Courage is being scared to death, but saddling up anyway." -- John Wayne

List 3 Things You're Grateful For Today

1	
2	
3	

Your Top 5 Long Term Goals (1-3 Years)

1	
2	
3	
4	
5	

The 5 Things You Aim To Accomplish Today

1		
2		
3		
4		
5		

Come Up With 5 Unique Ideas

1	
2	
3	
4	
5	

End Of The Day Reflections

Plan Out Your Day | Today's Date:

What's Your Why

_____
_____
_____

What do Elon Musk, Oprah, and a broke loser complaining about not finding a job have in common? They each get only 24 hours in a day. And so do you. So be sure to spend yours wisely!

12am	
1	
2	
3	
4	
5	
6	
7	
8	
9	
10	
11	
12pm	
1	
2	
3	
4	
5	
6	
7	
8	
9	
10	
11	

Quote Of The Day

"A good person dyes events with his own color...and turns whatever happens to his own benefit." - Seneca

List 3 Things You're Grateful For Today

1	
2	
3	

Your Top 5 Long Term Goals (1-3 Years)

1	
2	
3	
4	
5	

The 5 Things You Aim To Accomplish Today

1		
2		
3		
4		
5		

Come Up With 5 Unique Ideas

1	
2	
3	
4	
5	

End Of The Day Reflections

_____

_____

_____

_____

_____

_____

Plan Out Your Day | Today's Date:

What's Your Why

_____
_____
_____

What do Elon Musk, Oprah, and a broke loser complaining about not finding a job have in common? They each get only 24 hours in a day. And so do you. So be sure to spend yours wisely!

12am	
1	
2	
3	
4	
5	
6	
7	
8	
9	
10	
11	
12pm	
1	
2	
3	
4	
5	
6	
7	
8	
9	
10	
11	

Quote Of The Day
"Amateurs sit and wait for inspiration, the rest of us just get up and go to work." - Stephen King

List 3 Things You're Grateful For Today

1	
2	
3	

Your Top 5 Long Term Goals (1-3 Years)

1	
2	
3	
4	
5	

The 5 Things You Aim To Accomplish Today

1		
2		
3		
4		
5		

Come Up With 5 Unique Ideas

1	
2	
3	
4	
5	

End Of The Day Reflections

_____
_____
_____
_____
_____

Plan Out Your Day | Today's Date:

What's Your Why

_____
_____
_____

What do Elon Musk, Oprah, and a broke loser complaining about not finding a job have in common? They each get only 24 hours in a day. And so do you. So be sure to spend yours wisely!

12am	
1	
2	
3	
4	
5	
6	
7	
8	
9	
10	
11	
12pm	
1	
2	
3	
4	
5	
6	
7	
8	
9	
10	
11	

Quote Of The Day

"Second by second, you lose the opportunity to become the person you've always wanted to be. When are you going to stop making excuses, and take charge of your fucking life?" – Greg Plitt

List 3 Things You're Grateful For Today

1.
2.
3.

Your Top 5 Long Term Goals (1-3 Years)

1.
2.
3.
4.
5.

The 5 Things You Aim To Accomplish Today

1.
2.
3.
4.
5.

Come Up With 5 Unique Ideas

1.
2.
3.
4.
5.

End Of The Day Reflections

Plan Out Your Day | Today's Date:

What's Your Why

_____

_____

_____

What do Elon Musk, Oprah, and a broke loser complaining about not finding a job have in common? They each get only 24 hours in a day. And so do you. So be sure to spend yours wisely!

12am	
1	
2	
3	
4	
5	
6	
7	
8	
9	
10	
11	
12pm	
1	
2	
3	
4	
5	
6	
7	
8	
9	
10	
11	

Quote Of The Day
"I have been up against tough competition all my life. I wouldn't know how to get along without it." - Walt Disney

List 3 Things You're Grateful For Today

1	
2	
3	

Your Top 5 Long Term Goals (1-3 Years)

1	
2	
3	
4	
5	

The 5 Things You Aim To Accomplish Today

1		
2		
3		
4		
5		

Come Up With 5 Unique Ideas

1	
2	
3	
4	
5	

End Of The Day Reflections

Plan Out Your Day | Today's Date:

What's Your Why

_____
_____
_____

What do Elon Musk, Oprah, and a broke loser complaining about not finding a job have in common? They each get only 24 hours in a day. And so do you. So be sure to spend yours wisely!

12am	
1	
2	
3	
4	
5	
6	
7	
8	
9	
10	
11	
12pm	
1	
2	
3	
4	
5	
6	
7	
8	
9	
10	
11	

Quote Of The Day
"I have far more respect for the person with a single idea who gets there than for the person with a thousand ideas who does nothing." - Thomas Edison

List 3 Things You're Grateful For Today

1	
2	
3	

Your Top 5 Long Term Goals (1-3 Years)

1	
2	
3	
4	
5	

The 5 Things You Aim To Accomplish Today

1		
2		
3		
4		
5		

Come Up With 5 Unique Ideas

1	
2	
3	
4	
5	

End Of The Day Reflections

_____
_____
_____
_____
_____
_____

Plan Out Your Day | Today's Date:

What's Your Why

_____
_____
_____

What do Elon Musk, Oprah, and a broke loser complaining about not finding a job have in common? They each get only 24 hours in a day. And so do you. So be sure to spend yours wisely!

12am	
1	
2	
3	
4	
5	
6	
7	
8	
9	
10	
11	
12pm	
1	
2	
3	
4	
5	
6	
7	
8	
9	
10	
11	

Quote Of The Day
"If you're prepared and you know what it takes, it's not a risk. You just have to figure out how to get there. There is always a way to get there." - Mark Cuban

List 3 Things You're Grateful For Today

1	
2	
3	

Your Top 5 Long Term Goals (1-3 Years)

1	
2	
3	
4	
5	

The 5 Things You Aim To Accomplish Today

1		
2		
3		
4		
5		

Come Up With 5 Unique Ideas

1	
2	
3	
4	
5	

End Of The Day Reflections

_____
_____
_____
_____
_____
_____

Plan Out Your Day | Today's Date:

What's Your Why

_____
_____
_____

What do Elon Musk, Oprah, and a broke loser complaining about not finding a job have in common? They each get only 24 hours in a day. And so do you. So be sure to spend yours wisely!

12am	
1	
2	
3	
4	
5	
6	
7	
8	
9	
10	
11	
12pm	
1	
2	
3	
4	
5	
6	
7	
8	
9	
10	
11	

Quote Of The Day
"Experience is a school where a man learns what a big fool he has been." - Josh Billings

List 3 Things You're Grateful For Today

1	
2	
3	

Your Top 5 Long Term Goals (1-3 Years)

1	
2	
3	
4	
5	

The 5 Things You Aim To Accomplish Today

1		
2		
3		
4		
5		

Come Up With 5 Unique Ideas

1	
2	
3	
4	
5	

End Of The Day Reflections

Plan Out Your Day | Today's Date:

What's Your Why

_____
_____
_____

What do Elon Musk, Oprah, and a broke loser complaining about not finding a job have in common? They each get only 24 hours in a day. And so do you. So be sure to spend yours wisely!

12am	
1	
2	
3	
4	
5	
6	
7	
8	
9	
10	
11	
12pm	
1	
2	
3	
4	
5	
6	
7	
8	
9	
10	
11	

Quote Of The Day

"If you're going to be crazy, you have to get paid for it or else you're going to be locked up." – Hunter S. Thompson

List 3 Things You're Grateful For Today

1	
2	
3	

Your Top 5 Long Term Goals (1-3 Years)

1	
2	
3	
4	
5	

The 5 Things You Aim To Accomplish Today

1		
2		
3		
4		
5		

Come Up With 5 Unique Ideas

1	
2	
3	
4	
5	

End Of The Day Reflections

Plan Out Your Day | Today's Date:

What's Your Why

_____
_____
_____

What do Elon Musk, Oprah, and a broke loser complaining about not finding a job have in common? They each get only 24 hours in a day. And so do you. So be sure to spend yours wisely!

12am	
1	
2	
3	
4	
5	
6	
7	
8	
9	
10	
11	
12pm	
1	
2	
3	
4	
5	
6	
7	
8	
9	
10	
11	

Quote Of The Day
"The brave may not live forever, but the cautious do not live at all." - Richard Branson

List 3 Things You're Grateful For Today

1	
2	
3	

Your Top 5 Long Term Goals (1-3 Years)

1	
2	
3	
4	
5	

The 5 Things You Aim To Accomplish Today

1		
2		
3		
4		
5		

Come Up With 5 Unique Ideas

1	
2	
3	
4	
5	

End Of The Day Reflections

_____
_____
_____
_____
_____

Plan Out Your Day | Today's Date:

What's Your Why

_____
_____
_____

What do Elon Musk, Oprah, and a broke loser complaining about not finding a job have in common? They each get only 24 hours in a day. And so do you. So be sure to spend yours wisely!

12am	
1	
2	
3	
4	
5	
6	
7	
8	
9	
10	
11	
12pm	
1	
2	
3	
4	
5	
6	
7	
8	
9	
10	
11	

Quote Of The Day

"As I grow older I pay less attention to what men say. I just watch what they do." – Andrew Carnegie

List 3 Things You're Grateful For Today

1	
2	
3	

Your Top 5 Long Term Goals (1-3 Years)

1	
2	
3	
4	
5	

The 5 Things You Aim To Accomplish Today

1		
2		
3		
4		
5		

Come Up With 5 Unique Ideas

1	
2	
3	
4	
5	

End Of The Day Reflections

Plan Out Your Day | Today's Date:

What's Your Why

_____
_____
_____

What do Elon Musk, Oprah, and a broke loser complaining about not finding a job have in common? They each get only 24 hours in a day. And so do you. So be sure to spend yours wisely!

12am	
1	
2	
3	
4	
5	
6	
7	
8	
9	
10	
11	
12pm	
1	
2	
3	
4	
5	
6	
7	
8	
9	
10	
11	

Quote Of The Day
"Success in any field, but especially in business is about working with people, not against them." - Keith Ferrazzi

List 3 Things You're Grateful For Today

1	
2	
3	

Your Top 5 Long Term Goals (1-3 Years)

1	
2	
3	
4	
5	

The 5 Things You Aim To Accomplish Today

1		
2		
3		
4		
5		

Come Up With 5 Unique Ideas

1	
2	
3	
4	
5	

End Of The Day Reflections

_____

_____

_____

_____

Plan Out Your Day | Today's Date:

What's Your Why

_____
_____
_____

What do Elon Musk, Oprah, and a broke loser complaining about not finding a job have in common? They each get only 24 hours in a day. And so do you. So be sure to spend yours wisely!

12am	
1	
2	
3	
4	
5	
6	
7	
8	
9	
10	
11	
12pm	
1	
2	
3	
4	
5	
6	
7	
8	
9	
10	
11	

Quote Of The Day

"In my experience, successful people shoot for the stars, put their hearts on the line in every battle…In the long run, painful losses may prove much more valuable than wins… This, maybe our biggest hurdle, is at the core of the art of learning." - Joshua Waitzkin

List 3 Things You're Grateful For Today

1	
2	
3	

Your Top 5 Long Term Goals (1-3 Years)

1	
2	
3	
4	
5	

The 5 Things You Aim To Accomplish Today

1		
2		
3		
4		
5		

Come Up With 5 Unique Ideas

1	
2	
3	
4	
5	

End Of The Day Reflections

_____
_____
_____
_____
_____
_____

Plan Out Your Day | Today's Date:

What's Your Why

_____
_____
_____

What do Elon Musk, Oprah, and a broke loser complaining about not finding a job have in common? They each get only 24 hours in a day. And so do you. So be sure to spend yours wisely!

12am	
1	
2	
3	
4	
5	
6	
7	
8	
9	
10	
11	
12pm	
1	
2	
3	
4	
5	
6	
7	
8	
9	
10	
11	

Quote Of The Day
"I want to be remembered as a person who wasn't afraid to start things." - Tina Roth Eisenberg

List 3 Things You're Grateful For Today

1	
2	
3	

Your Top 5 Long Term Goals (1-3 Years)

1	
2	
3	
4	
5	

The 5 Things You Aim To Accomplish Today

1		
2		
3		
4		
5		

Come Up With 5 Unique Ideas

1	
2	
3	
4	
5	

End Of The Day Reflections

_____
_____
_____
_____
_____

Plan Out Your Day | Today's Date:

What's Your Why

_____
_____
_____

What do Elon Musk, Oprah, and a broke loser complaining about not finding a job have in common? They each get only 24 hours in a day. And so do you. So be sure to spend yours wisely!

12am	
1	
2	
3	
4	
5	
6	
7	
8	
9	
10	
11	
12pm	
1	
2	
3	
4	
5	
6	
7	
8	
9	
10	
11	

Quote Of The Day
"To live is the rarest thing in the world. Most people exist, that is all." - Oscar Wilde

List 3 Things You're Grateful For Today

1	
2	
3	

Your Top 5 Long Term Goals (1-3 Years)

1	
2	
3	
4	
5	

The 5 Things You Aim To Accomplish Today

1		
2		
3		
4		
5		

Come Up With 5 Unique Ideas

1	
2	
3	
4	
5	

End Of The Day Reflections

_____
_____
_____
_____
_____

Plan Out Your Day | Today's Date:

What's Your Why

_____
_____
_____

What do Elon Musk, Oprah, and a broke loser complaining about not finding a job have in common? They each get only 24 hours in a day. And so do you. So be sure to spend yours wisely!

12am	
1	
2	
3	
4	
5	
6	
7	
8	
9	
10	
11	
12pm	
1	
2	
3	
4	
5	
6	
7	
8	
9	
10	
11	

Quote Of The Day
"The fear of death follows from the fear of life. A man who lives fully is prepared to die at any time." -- Mark Twain

List 3 Things You're Grateful For Today

1	
2	
3	

Your Top 5 Long Term Goals (1-3 Years)

1	
2	
3	
4	
5	

The 5 Things You Aim To Accomplish Today

1		
2		
3		
4		
5		

Come Up With 5 Unique Ideas

1	
2	
3	
4	
5	

End Of The Day Reflections

_____
_____
_____
_____
_____

Plan Out Your Day | Today's Date:

What's Your Why

_____
_____
_____

What do Elon Musk, Oprah, and a broke loser complaining about not finding a job have in common? They each get only 24 hours in a day. And so do you. So be sure to spend yours wisely!

12am	
1	
2	
3	
4	
5	
6	
7	
8	
9	
10	
11	
12pm	
1	
2	
3	
4	
5	
6	
7	
8	
9	
10	
11	

Quote Of The Day

"The moment that you feel that, just possibly, you're walking down the street naked, exposing too much of your heart and your mind and what exists on the inside, showing too much of yourself. That's the moment you may be starting to get it right." - Neil Gaiman

List 3 Things You're Grateful For Today

1	
2	
3	

Your Top 5 Long Term Goals (1-3 Years)

1	
2	
3	
4	
5	

The 5 Things You Aim To Accomplish Today

1		
2		
3		
4		
5		

Come Up With 5 Unique Ideas

1	
2	
3	
4	
5	

End Of The Day Reflections

_____
_____
_____
_____
_____
_____

Plan Out Your Day | Today's Date:

What's Your Why

_____
_____
_____

What do Elon Musk, Oprah, and a broke loser complaining about not finding a job have in common? They each get only 24 hours in a day. And so do you. So be sure to spend yours wisely!

12am	
1	
2	
3	
4	
5	
6	
7	
8	
9	
10	
11	
12pm	
1	
2	
3	
4	
5	
6	
7	
8	
9	
10	
11	

Quote Of The Day

"Building a business from scratch is 24 hours, 7 days a week, divorces, it's difficult to hold your family life together, it's bloody hard work and only one word really matters — and that's surviving." -- Richard Branson

List 3 Things You're Grateful For Today

1	
2	
3	

Your Top 5 Long Term Goals (1-3 Years)

1	
2	
3	
4	
5	

The 5 Things You Aim To Accomplish Today

1		
2		
3		
4		
5		

Come Up With 5 Unique Ideas

1	
2	
3	
4	
5	

End Of The Day Reflections

_____

_____

_____

_____

_____

Plan Out Your Day | Today's Date:

What's Your Why

_____
_____
_____

What do Elon Musk, Oprah, and a broke loser complaining about not finding a job have in common? They each get only 24 hours in a day. And so do you. So be sure to spend yours wisely!

12am	
1	
2	
3	
4	
5	
6	
7	
8	
9	
10	
11	
12pm	
1	
2	
3	
4	
5	
6	
7	
8	
9	
10	
11	

Quote Of The Day
"I only want people around me who can do the impossible." - Elizabeth Arden

List 3 Things You're Grateful For Today

1	
2	
3	

Your Top 5 Long Term Goals (1-3 Years)

1	
2	
3	
4	
5	

The 5 Things You Aim To Accomplish Today

1		
2		
3		
4		
5		

Come Up With 5 Unique Ideas

1	
2	
3	
4	
5	

End Of The Day Reflections

_____
_____
_____
_____
_____
_____

Plan Out Your Day | Today's Date:

What's Your Why

_____

_____

_____

What do Elon Musk, Oprah, and a broke loser complaining about not finding a job have in common? They each get only 24 hours in a day. And so do you. So be sure to spend yours wisely!

12am	
1	
2	
3	
4	
5	
6	
7	
8	
9	
10	
11	
12pm	
1	
2	
3	
4	
5	
6	
7	
8	
9	
10	
11	

Quote Of The Day

"The more you say, the more likely you are to blow past opportunities, ignore feedback and reveal weaknesses before you've had a chance to work on them. Because you're too busy talking to hear any of it." - Ryan Holiday

List 3 Things You're Grateful For Today

1	
2	
3	

Your Top 5 Long Term Goals (1-3 Years)

1	
2	
3	
4	
5	

The 5 Things You Aim To Accomplish Today

1		
2		
3		
4		
5		

Come Up With 5 Unique Ideas

1	
2	
3	
4	
5	

End Of The Day Reflections

Plan Out Your Day | Today's Date:

What's Your Why

_____
_____
_____

What do Elon Musk, Oprah, and a broke loser complaining about not finding a job have in common? They each get only 24 hours in a day. And so do you. So be sure to spend yours wisely!

12am	
1	
2	
3	
4	
5	
6	
7	
8	
9	
10	
11	
12pm	
1	
2	
3	
4	
5	
6	
7	
8	
9	
10	
11	

Quote Of The Day
"Among my most prized possessions are words that I have never spoken." — Orson Scott Card

List 3 Things You're Grateful For Today

1	
2	
3	

Your Top 5 Long Term Goals (1-3 Years)

1	
2	
3	
4	
5	

The 5 Things You Aim To Accomplish Today

1		
2		
3		
4		
5		

Come Up With 5 Unique Ideas

1	
2	
3	
4	
5	

End Of The Day Reflections

_____
_____
_____
_____
_____

Plan Out Your Day | Today's Date:

What's Your Why

_____
_____
_____

What do Elon Musk, Oprah, and a broke loser complaining about not finding a job have in common? They each get only 24 hours in a day. And so do you. So be sure to spend yours wisely!

12am	
1	
2	
3	
4	
5	
6	
7	
8	
9	
10	
11	
12pm	
1	
2	
3	
4	
5	
6	
7	
8	
9	
10	
11	

Quote Of The Day
"Never tell your problems to anyone…20% don't care and the other 80% are glad you have them." - Lou Holtz

List 3 Things You're Grateful For Today

1	
2	
3	

Your Top 5 Long Term Goals (1-3 Years)

1	
2	
3	
4	
5	

The 5 Things You Aim To Accomplish Today

1		
2		
3		
4		
5		

Come Up With 5 Unique Ideas

1	
2	
3	
4	
5	

End Of The Day Reflections

Plan Out Your Day | Today's Date:

What's Your Why

_____
_____
_____

What do Elon Musk, Oprah, and a broke loser complaining about not finding a job have in common? They each get only 24 hours in a day. And so do you. So be sure to spend yours wisely!

12am	
1	
2	
3	
4	
5	
6	
7	
8	
9	
10	
11	
12pm	
1	
2	
3	
4	
5	
6	
7	
8	
9	
10	
11	

Quote Of The Day

"If you don't ship, you actually haven't started anything at all. At some point, your work has to intersect with the market. At some point, you need feedback as to whether or not it worked. Otherwise, it's merely a hobby." - Seth Godin

List 3 Things You're Grateful For Today

1	
2	
3	

Your Top 5 Long Term Goals (1-3 Years)

1	
2	
3	
4	
5	

The 5 Things You Aim To Accomplish Today

1		
2		
3		
4		
5		

Come Up With 5 Unique Ideas

1	
2	
3	
4	
5	

End Of The Day Reflections

_____
_____
_____
_____
_____

Plan Out Your Day | Today's Date:

What's Your Why

_____
_____
_____

What do Elon Musk, Oprah, and a broke loser complaining about not finding a job have in common? They each get only 24 hours in a day. And so do you. So be sure to spend yours wisely!

12am	
1	
2	
3	
4	
5	
6	
7	
8	
9	
10	
11	
12pm	
1	
2	
3	
4	
5	
6	
7	
8	
9	
10	
11	

Quote Of The Day

"Much talking is the cause of danger. Silence is the means of avoiding misfortune. The talkative parrot is shut up in a cage. Other birds, without speech, fly freely about." - Saskya Pandita

List 3 Things You're Grateful For Today

1	
2	
3	

Your Top 5 Long Term Goals (1-3 Years)

1	
2	
3	
4	
5	

The 5 Things You Aim To Accomplish Today

1		
2		
3		
4		
5		

Come Up With 5 Unique Ideas

1	
2	
3	
4	
5	

End Of The Day Reflections

_____
_____
_____
_____
_____

Plan Out Your Day | Today's Date:

What's Your Why

_____
_____
_____

What do Elon Musk, Oprah, and a broke loser complaining about not finding a job have in common? They each get only 24 hours in a day. And so do you. So be sure to spend yours wisely!

12am	
1	
2	
3	
4	
5	
6	
7	
8	
9	
10	
11	
12pm	
1	
2	
3	
4	
5	
6	
7	
8	
9	
10	
11	

Quote Of The Day
"Life is either a daring adventure or nothing at all." - Hellen Keller

List 3 Things You're Grateful For Today

1	
2	
3	

Your Top 5 Long Term Goals (1-3 Years)

1	
2	
3	
4	
5	

The 5 Things You Aim To Accomplish Today

1		
2		
3		
4		
5		

Come Up With 5 Unique Ideas

1	
2	
3	
4	
5	

End Of The Day Reflections

_____
_____
_____
_____
_____

Plan Out Your Day | Today's Date:

What's Your Why

_____
_____
_____

What do Elon Musk, Oprah, and a broke loser complaining about not finding a job have in common? They each get only 24 hours in a day. And so do you. So be sure to spend yours wisely!

12am	
1	
2	
3	
4	
5	
6	
7	
8	
9	
10	
11	
12pm	
1	
2	
3	
4	
5	
6	
7	
8	
9	
10	
11	

Quote Of The Day

"If you end up with a boring miserable life because you listened to your mom, your dad, your teacher, your priest, or some guy on television telling you how to do your shit, then you deserve it." — Frank Zappa

List 3 Things You're Grateful For Today

1	
2	
3	

Your Top 5 Long Term Goals (1-3 Years)

1	
2	
3	
4	
5	

The 5 Things You Aim To Accomplish Today

1		
2		
3		
4		
5		

Come Up With 5 Unique Ideas

1	
2	
3	
4	
5	

End Of The Day Reflections

_____
_____
_____
_____
_____

Plan Out Your Day | Today's Date:

What's Your Why

_____
_____
_____

What do Elon Musk, Oprah, and a broke loser complaining about not finding a job have in common? They each get only 24 hours in a day. And so do you. So be sure to spend yours wisely!

12am	
1	
2	
3	
4	
5	
6	
7	
8	
9	
10	
11	
12pm	
1	
2	
3	
4	
5	
6	
7	
8	
9	
10	
11	

Quote Of The Day
"Either you run the day or the day runs you" - Jim Rohn

List 3 Things You're Grateful For Today

1	
2	
3	

Your Top 5 Long Term Goals (1-3 Years)

1	
2	
3	
4	
5	

The 5 Things You Aim To Accomplish Today

1		
2		
3		
4		
5		

Come Up With 5 Unique Ideas

1	
2	
3	
4	
5	

End Of The Day Reflections

_____

_____

_____

_____

_____

Plan Out Your Day | Today's Date:

What's Your Why

_____
_____
_____

What do Elon Musk, Oprah, and a broke loser complaining about not finding a job have in common? They each get only 24 hours in a day. And so do you. So be sure to spend yours wisely!

12am	
1	
2	
3	
4	
5	
6	
7	
8	
9	
10	
11	
12pm	
1	
2	
3	
4	
5	
6	
7	
8	
9	
10	
11	

Quote Of The Day

"There are no traffic jams along the extra mile" – Roger Staubach

List 3 Things You're Grateful For Today

1	
2	
3	

Your Top 5 Long Term Goals (1-3 Years)

1	
2	
3	
4	
5	

The 5 Things You Aim To Accomplish Today

1		
2		
3		
4		
5		

Come Up With 5 Unique Ideas

1	
2	
3	
4	
5	

End Of The Day Reflections

_____
_____
_____
_____
_____
_____

Plan Out Your Day | Today's Date:

What's Your Why

_____
_____
_____

What do Elon Musk, Oprah, and a broke loser complaining about not finding a job have in common? They each get only 24 hours in a day. And so do you. So be sure to spend yours wisely!

12am	
1	
2	
3	
4	
5	
6	
7	
8	
9	
10	
11	
12pm	
1	
2	
3	
4	
5	
6	
7	
8	
9	
10	
11	

Congrats, You Made It! Here's What To Do Next...

Believe it or not, making it to 60 days is *huge* accomplishment. Most can't even hold themselves accountable for a week and yet here you are, 8 weeks later, sticking to the grind, and charging full steam ahead towards your goals.

We hope this planner helped you accomplish what you set out to accomplish.

But remember, your long term goals still need you to keep up the hustle. At this point, here are the two things you should do to keep yourself motivated and keep the "chain" going.

Step 1: Order more copies of this planner. Go on Amazon, or head over to the link below, and order 3-5 copies so that your following months are covered! (Order here: www.doyouevenhustle.net/planner)

Step 2: Go over your last 60 days to find trends. Actions prove who someone is, words prove who they *want* to be. Did you accomplish your 5 daily tasks with consistency? Or did you just write them down, and then get distracted? What about your long term goals? Did you start off dreaming big, only to end off your 60 days with small minded thinking? If so, you need to cut that out and aim higher. It can be very liberating to see how your old self compares to the new you.

Step 3: Read the Bonus Section on the next page. This is where you'll find 31 of the most proven ways to keep yourself motivated. You may have gone through this list in the past, but it helps to go over it again and try out some of the techniques that you never got around to trying.

Bonus: 31 Ways To Stay Motivated

1 – Keep Up The "Chain"

One of the most deceiving things about motivation, is that those who already have it, get more of it without much effort. It's like the snowball effect; you start small, but as you keep rolling that ball of clumped up snowflakes down a hill, it gets bigger and bigger. It builds momentum, and before you know it, you have a 400 pound ball of ice that is near unstoppable.

The problem is, if that 400 pound ice ball *does* come to a halt, you're going to have one hell of a time getting it rolling again. That's why we encourage you to stick to this planner for 60 days in a row. Each day is like a link in the chain. Your job is to **not** break the chain, and *trust* the process. You know who else operates this way?

Jerry Seinfeld. He has a massive calendar on his wall, and every day he writes jokes down on a piece of paper. When he does, he marks his calendar with an "X" and keeps this chain going for as long as possible. If you doubt this method, just know that he's only worth about... **800 million** dollars!

2 – Add An <u>EXTRA</u> 10% To Everything You Do

Just when you think you've crossed your finish line, we want you to make it a habit of giving just a little bit more. Did 10 pushups? Good add just one more. Gave a homeless guy $5? Screw it, give him one more. When you get into a habit of adding 10% to everything in your life, it all adds up to you living a live that's eventually 100% better. This planner is the perfect example – we thought we were done with it after the 60 days of space that you get to write everything down.

Then I was like, *"you know, we should probably give away 10 of our best motivation secrets incase people have a really shitty day. It'll be a valuable tool."* To which Martin responded with, *"why just 10? I have many more. Let's make it 20!"*. Then after 20, I realized there are 11 more which I thought you could benefit from. And so here we are, with a grand-total of 31. Not only do you get more value for your money, but our brand ends up with a far superior product which we are proud to offer to the world. And we can tell you from first-hand experience that this is very motivating indeed!

3 – Raise Your Skills Instead Of Worrying About Your Fear

If we were at a bar right now, and told you to approach the most beautiful stranger and ask for their number, would you do it? Gentlemen, do you have the balls to approach that *stunner* who's surrounded by two other dudes? Ladies, are you confident enough to go after a man who already "seems" to be talking to another beautiful woman? Or what about if we asked you to go door to door, and sell a box of chocolates to strangers?

If any of these tasks make you nervous or drive fear into your bones, that's because your skill level is too low. Regardless of your job, or task at hand, just remember that when your skill level rises, the corresponding fear level drops. Speak in front of a crowd the first time, and it'll be scary as hell. But by the 100th time, it'll be a walk in the park. A great skillset will drive up your confidence through the roof, which in turn will keep your motivation at an all-time high!

4 – Give, Without Expecting Something In Return

One of the most sleaze-ball things you can do is *pretend* to offer help to someone, only to "cash in" the favor at a later date. Not only does this ruin friendships and relationships, but people will generally despise you because they'll know you always have an agenda. Now don't get us wrong, there are certainly times where a transaction such as *"you scratch my back, and I scratch yours"* is warranted.

But if that's what you want, ask for it and be clear about your intentions. Be straight up. However, that's not always motivating. Sometimes it can feel like a necessity. Instead, Try giving without expecting anything. This will force you to live in a mindset of abundance, and make someone happy… which as far as we know, has *never* failed to energize and motivate an individual.

Want an easy way to do this? Buy 10 copies of this planner, and give it away to those you think will find it useful. In fact, we constantly give away our highest priced products and services to friends and family without expecting anything. This builds lots of trust and on the plus side, positions us as the experts in our field. This brings in referrals, which brings in money and attention… and what hustler doesn't find that motivating? We sure do!

5 - Set Achievable Daily Tasks

If you want to become the best punk rock DJ in your community, it won't happen overnight. The large goal itself may drive you, but if you keep focusing on it, it can also become intimidating. The best thing to do, is focus on the **next logical step**, such as figuring out which electronic mix table to get. Or learn how to scratch like a champ! And every time you achieve these daily tasks, it will boost confidence and motivate you.

6 - Forget Multi-Tasking. Focus On One Thing At A Time

It's tempting to start thinking about the future, or the vast number of things you want to finish. Instead, focus **only** on the task at hand. Don't worry about the whole season, worry about the next play.

We apply this logic to blogging, working out, and even growing our podcast. You can't stress about why you don't have a six pack yet. All you can do is focus on your next set to ensure that you get the best possible workout in today.

7 - Keep A Picture Of Your Desired Result Around

"Why do you have a picture of a Hummer in your locker?"

Martin asked a buddy of his many years ago. He responded by telling him that he wanted to buy one. Whenever he lost focus, was having a bad day at work, or felt like slacking off, he would open up his locker to see this picture. He would then be reminded of why he was working and saving up. He really wanted that vehicle. And guess what? He ended up buying it.

Coincidence?

We think not.

8 - Let The World Know

Let your friends know about what you're working on. Keep everyone in the loop. Post about your goals on your social media accounts. This will force you to be held accountable. You can't miss that workout when all of your friends know that you're trying to get in shape.

9 - Reward Yourself

Are you rewarding yourself? Life can be tough. This is why it's important to be rewarding yourself constantly. Celebrate the little wins. Treat yourself to a new cup of coffee or go for dinner at your favorite restaurant. It's tempting to go "beast mode" all the time but it can be exhausting. Being burnt-out is a real phenomenon. Avoid it all costs.

10 – Surround Yourself With Winners

Why do you think rich, successful entrepreneurs hang around other rich, successful entrepreneurs? Or why celebrities hang around and spend time with other celebrities. Hell, successful people even go out of their way to live amongst each other. Success attracts more success and poverty attracts more poverty. It's a shame, but such is the way life works.

That's why it's so difficult to "break out" when you're in the lower rungs of the ladder. It takes a tremendous amount of energy to climb to the top. But one way to make it easier, is to climb a ladder beside those that have already made the climb. That's why apprenticeships were so common place hundreds of years ago.

Disciples that hung around great artists, became great artists themselves. Those that hung around great scientists, became great scientists.

We're not saying that if you hang around billionaires that you'll become one, but chances are very high that you'll at least become a millionaire at the very least. That's how osmosis works. And its effects are *very* real.

11 - Make It Fun/Gamify The Goal

We all get bored at some point. Working out and eating healthy gets annoying. This is why you have to make it fun. Stop being so boring about everything. Turn your goals in a game. Make things fun. Give yourself points for every time you accomplish something. The "chain" system we talked about is this technique in full effect.

Make it so that every time you successfully have a 10-link chain, you reward yourself with a massage, pedicure or even just a simple movie.

12 - Think Of The Finish Line

[Martin] Whenever I help someone with a goal I try to remind them of the finish line. I helped a reader pay off over $40k worth of debt. Besides giving her the tools to succeed, the only other thing I did was *constantly* remind her of the finish line. This made the long days worth it.

13 - Surround Yourself With Positive People

Stop hanging out with losers. We've all heard that line about how you should never be the smartest person in the room. You should hang out with people better than you. Surround yourself with positive folks and you'll never run out of motivation. Stop hanging out with the same negative whiners.

14 - Don't Take Advice From Quitters

You should never take advice from someone unless you're willing to trade places with them. Nor should you take advice from anyone who talks like a big shot, but just can't seem to finish anything. Don't let someone that failed or give up bring you down. We often lose motivation because we listen to those that couldn't cut it. You want motivation? Write an article, go on Medium.com and publish it to the world. Even if 3 people read it, who cares?

The bottom line is that you shipped! You put something out there. You finished. That's better than 90% of people who never even get to the finish line, yet have the balls to give advice. You know what? Fuck those people. You don't need such mediocrity in your life. We would rather listen to someone who crossed the finish line in 5th place over and over, than someone who never crossed the finish line at all.

15 - Sleep On It

A lack of sleep will kill all of your motivation and make you miserable. As hustlers, we're used to bragging about how little sleep we get. It can be a badge of honor. But doing week-long marathons on little sleep can only last for so long. Sleep deprivation is not a winning **long term** strategy. Now, we look forward to sleeping in. You need your rest. If you're not feeling motivated, you could simply be in some desperate need of rest. Pass out, and wake up refreshed. Or you can use the power of accumulation and take naps.

It doesn't matter how you slice it, if you can get 8 hours of *quality* rest within a 24 hour window, you'll perform at your best.

16 - Keep An Inspirational Playlist

[Martin] This is so corny but I remember making a playlist of all of those motivational mixes off YouTube when I first ran a half-marathon. These songs really got me going. A simple search of "motivational playlist" will help you find some inspirational videos. YouTube will then suggest many other videos. Check them out and get pumped.

17 – Measure Your Most Important Metrics

If you don't know how to use Excel, find some YouTube videos and learn it. You don't have to get fancy. All you need to know is how to input 2 sets of data (numbers) and create a graph. That's it. Now start tracking 2 or 3 of the most important metrics and review them weekly. If you have an online business, track your traffic, sales and email opt-in rate. If you're a powerlifter, measure your progress on the squat, bench and deadlift. If you want to lose weight, track your daily food intake and calories. Numbers charted on a graph do two things:

i. They don't lie.

ii. They reveal a trend.

It's quite motivating when you see a sales graph trending in the upward direction, week after week. Trust us!

18 - Watch An Acceptance Speech

You know what gets us going? Watching retirement speeches, acceptance speeches, or even TED talks. [Martin] I've been on a huge kick of wrestling retirement speeches lately. They really get me going because they show me what's at the finish line.

Watch a speech and see how you feel after. Or hell, even a TED talk will do. (Pro Tip: while original TED talks are great, look for talks from TEDx and TED-ed events. They're absolute gold!)

19 - Remember Why You Started

If you recall, in the very beginning we asked you to complete two steps: go on the information diet, and find out your why. But it's natural to forget your reasoning sometimes. So take some time to reflect on it again: Why did you start? Whenever you lose motivation please remember why you started. Whenever I get lazy during a workout I remind myself of why I'm even here at the gym in the first place.

20 - Turn Off Social Media And Go Outside

Yes, you can go outside. You'll find plenty of motivation by going for a bike ride or a walk in the park. Get out there and see what the world has to offer. Don't sit around on social media waiting for motivation to hit you. **Motion creates emotion.** When you start moving, and breathe in some fresh air, your head will clear and you'll come up with ideas you couldn't have thought of before. This will drive up you creative juices and motivate you to get shit done.

21 - Set A Small Quota

When you're focusing on the goal, I want you to set a small quota. We sometimes lose motivation because we get overwhelmed with what we have to do. For example, when I sat down to write this list of 20 ways to stay motivated, I told myself that I would write a list of five today, then five tomorrow etc. But as I started writing, I couldn't stop. Neither could Sahil, and here we are with 31 of the most bad-ass ways to stay motivated.

22 - Take The Weekend Off

The best thing for you sometimes is a weekend off. Invite some friends over, put on Saved By The Bell, order some pizza and let the good times begin. Get some rest so that you're not always over worked and stressed out.

"The foundations of good health are good diet, good exercise and good sleep, but two out of three doesn't get you there." -- Dr. Anne Calhoun

According to Harvard, the consequences of no- sleep are:

"In the short term, a lack of adequate sleep can affect judgment, mood, ability to learn and retain information, and may increase the risk of serious

accidents and injury. In the long term, chronic sleep deprivation may lead to a host of health problems including obesity, diabetes, cardiovascular disease, and even early mortality."

Don't listen to your buddy who brags about how little sleep he got this week. Once in a while it's ok, but doing it all the time isn't "hardcore". It's not cool. You need rest. It's okay to take the weekend off.

23 - Visualize Achieving It

Pretend you've already made it; that you're already in shape, that you're already a successful freelancer, that your podcast is #1. Now wake up and go after it.

Now we realize that we're not experts on this topic, or in neuroscience... **we just know that it works**. However, Jack Canfield definitely is an expert, and here's how he describes visualization on his website:

"Visualization is really quite simple. You sit in a comfortable position, close your eyes and imagine — in as vivid detail as you can — what you would be looking at if the dream you have were already realized. Imagine being inside of yourself, looking out through your eyes at the ideal result." http://jackcanfield.com/visualize-and-affirm-your-desired-outcomes-a-step-by-step-guide/

24 - Drink Coffee

We couldn't write a list about motivation without mentioning coffee. When all else fails, grab a cup of coffee and let the buzz kick in. How do you think we finished this planner? Also, below you will find Sahil's performance coffee recipe (he uses this with his top end athletes such as Record holding powerlifters, and World level gymnasts)

- 1.5 Tbsp Ground Coffee
- 1-2 Tbsp Raw Sugar (or sweetener of choice)
- 1 Piece Dark Chocolate (70% or higher)
- 1 Omega 3 Fortified Egg

- 1 Tsp Salt-Free Butter
- ½ Tsp Ground Cinnamon
- ½ Scoop Chocolate Whey Protein
- 1 Cup 2% Milk

Pour 1 cup boiling water in blender. Add in all the ingredients except the milk. Start blender on low setting and wait for ingredients to mix. Slowly pour in the milk. Once everything is in, ensure lid is tightly secure then blend on highest setting for 30 seconds. Pour and enjoy!

25 – Get A Mentor Or Ask For Advice From A Proven Winner

We're not talking about fly-by-night "life coaches" here. We mean reach out to someone who has achieved *exactly* the type of success you want, and ask them for guidance, or even just brutal feedback. Basically, seek out someone that has their shit together. Now the caveat is that **you need to keep asking** until someone responds and helps you. Because if you contact three people and all three turn you down, it can actually be de-motivating.

But trust us, the day you get someone you respect to truly help you out, you'll be over the moon! We have personally reached out to our favorite authors, entrepreneurs, and top level coaches for guidance. And you know what we found? They were *happy* to give back! Just be sure not to insult them by failing to applying their recommendations. When someone with a lot of success gives you advice, the best thing you can do is apply it and report back with results. By doing this, they'll remember you as someone who *actually* gets things done, and be open to helping you again in the future.

26 – Create A New Friend

Ever wonder why some celebrities end up cheating on their near "perfect" spouses? I mean Brad Pitt had Jennifer Aniston at one point, who (we think) is still a legitimate hottie. Now sure, you could argue that Angelina Jolie is hotter, but we think there's more to it than that. There is something motivating and exciting about connecting with a new person. Now obviously, we don't mean make a new friend *with benefits* (though if you're single and in a position to do so, then go for it). But more along the lines of, **make a new friend that has similar interests to your own**.

Every person on this Earth has lived through experiences that are unique to themselves, and thus they can come up with new perspectives that you probably never thought of before. Being in such company can really be motivating and energizing. Believe it or not, Martin & I have only been friends for just over a year... but it was bromance at the first banter. We feed off each other's ideas and motivate each other on the daily. Everything about the **Do You Even Hustle** brand is a joint-effort that resulted from exchanging ideas between two new friends.

27 – Host A Party

At a deep, subconscious level, all humans crave praise. We crave love and affection. Even if someone is "hard" and "bad-ass" on the exterior, they actually feel good when someone gives them a compliment, or praises their skills. But the life of a true hustler is littered with hard knocks, criticisms, and tough love. It has to be. However, it doesn't hurt now and again to be liked on some level. And the easiest way to do this, is to make sure everyone around you has a reason to have a good time.

So throw a party. A summer barbecue. A get together. A happy hour. Why? No reason. Just because. Get everyone together and have a good time. No one in the history of partying has ever gone up to a host and said, *"hey, I'm having a great time... screw you for throwing such a good party!"*

It's all praises, high-fives and an instant status boost. And that feels pretty damn good.

28 – Read One Non-Fiction Book Every Month

We've said this before on the podcast, but it bears repeating: one of the most valuable investments you can make, is in yourself. Just by buying this planner, you've already proven that you are always willing to upgrade your life. That's good. But the key is to never stop. If you hop over to our Instagram account and scroll down a little, you'll find an entire column of books we recommend.

We call this list "Essential Reading For Hustlers". These are all books we've personally read and can vouch for. They are educating, motivating and the absolute cream of the crop. Buy them, read them, apply them.

29 – Hit The Gym & Lift Weights

It doesn't matter if you're a 21 year old college dude, or a 45 year old mom with 3 kids. You need to hit the gym, and lift some weights. Start with 10 pounds if you have to, but lift it. Then do it again. If you want a proper workout plan, download our **Hustler's Success Kit** if you haven't already done so – it contains Sahil's BIG 5 workout that he uses with his clients to get them in incredible shape with just 5 exercises.

Video demonstrations are included. Grab the success kit here:
www.doyouevenhustle.net/success-kit

Trust us, when you're constantly squatting, deadlifting or pressing more weight every week, your strength and confidence will spill over into all other areas of your life. Lean, toned muscles will be built. Fat will be burnt off. Compliments from people will start coming your way, and your motivation will go from a small withering flame, to a raging volcano.

30 – Do The Most Difficult Things First

That's right, bite down on the biggest piece first. You can chew on the little nuggets later. Everything you do has an energy cost. Big tasks obviously take more energy than small tasks. And at what time are your energy levels at their highest? When you wake up, duh! For most people, this is in the morning.

For Martin and I, this means 11 or noon. Either way, the first thing you should do after waking up (besides filling out your planner) is tackle your biggest task out of the 5 that you write down. Don't put it off till later. If there's one thing we've learned, it's that procrastination feeds negativity, which eventually suffocates and destroys motivation levels.

31 – Get Laid

Ever noticed how **no one** wakes up in a bad mood after a night of passionate love making? Like, ever.

In fact, it's near impossible to become depressed in such a state. Also, if you get technical and look at sex from a biological stand point, you'll find that there are absolutely zero downsides to it. Don't believe us? Let's take a look (feel free to ask any medical doctor on Earth to verify this list, by the way): Burns calories, releases feel-good hormones, increases blood flow, boosts immune function, boosts testosterone (in both men and women!), lowers blood pressure, reduces pain, improves quality of sleep, speeds up recovery... shall we go on?

We think you get the point. And if you're a man that needs a willing partner, then you should definitely check out Martin's book, *I Like You As a Friend: How You Can Avoid The Friend Zone Forever.* It's available on Amazon, and you will love it.

Ladies, a willing partner for you is so easy that we're not going to get into it. And no, you're not a "slut" if you like sex. You're a human being with needs. Don't be afraid of breaking a few hearts. Real hustlers can handle it – we promise!

Final Thoughts

You owe it to yourself to use this planner and to take it seriously. Remember, hope is never a good game plan. **Action is always the answer.**

Buy a pack of high quality pens - ones that produce the smoothest stream of ink on a piece of paper. Turn writing down your goals and dreams into a joyous occasion.

Start from nothing and stop for nothing.

And if this planner helped you, buy a few copies and gift it to your friends and family members. Push people around you to step their game up. Because at the end of the day, who do you want to be surrounded by?

Wanna-be's and has-been's?

Or straight up winners and hustlers that strive to achieve something significant in their life?

We'll take the latter any day of the week.

Finally, don't forget to email us with your thoughts on the planner (we read every single email): **info@doyouevenhustle.net**

Hustle hard, go after your goals, and refuse to be average!

Sahil Mulla & Martin Dasko
Do You Even Hustle Podcast

      Order Additional Copies Of The Planner At The Link Below...
            www.doyouevenhustle.net/planner

Notes

Notes

Notes

Notes

Notes

Notes

Notes

Made in the USA
Lexington, KY
17 July 2017